101 Ultimate Tax Secrets Revealed

2013/14

By

Sarah Bradford

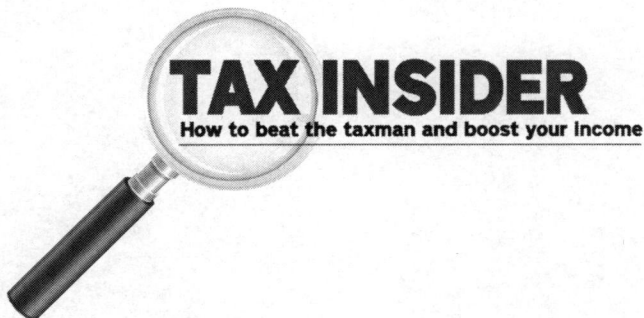

TAX INSIDER

How to beat the taxman and boost your income

Publisher Details

This guide is published by Tax Insider Ltd, 3 Sanderson Close, Great Sankey, Warrington WA5 3LN.

'101 Ultimate Tax Secrets Revealed' first published in July 2010, second edition September 2010, third edition May 2011, fourth edition April 2012, fifth edition May 2012, sixth edition August 2012, seventh edition April 2013.

Contents

Contents

Contents

Contents

Contents

Chapter 1.
Making the Most of Allowances and Lower Rates of Tax

1.   Use Non-Taxpayers' Personal Allowances

2.   Keeping The Full Personal Allowance

3.   Age-Related Tax Allowances

4.   Utilising Your Annual CGT Exemption

5.   Utilising Spouse's Or Civil Partner's Annual CGT Exemption

6.   Equalising Marginal Rates Of Tax

1.　Use Non-Taxpayers' Personal Allowances

If one spouse or civil partner is working and the other has no taxable income, it is worthwhile considering transferring income-producing investments to the non-working spouse/civil partner in order to utilise their personal allowance.

This will save tax on the income and will increase the overall return from these investments.

This can be useful with even the smallest amounts of savings.

> **Use Non-Taxpayers' Allowances**
>
> Mr and Mrs Smith have £25,000 in savings. The entire amount is held in Mr Smith's sole name.
>
> Mr Smith is a higher rate taxpayer and pays tax at 40%. Mrs Smith does not work and has no taxable income.
>
> At present, the interest received of £500 suffers tax at 40%, leaving a net amount received of £300.
>
> By transferring this money into an account in Mrs Smith's name and utilising her personal allowance, the interest can be received free of tax.
>
> This means that an instant tax saving of £200 can be made.

2.   Keeping The Full Personal Allowance

The basic personal allowance is reduced where a person has 'net adjusted income' in excess of £100,000. The personal allowance (£9,440 for 2013/14) is reduced by £1 for every £2 by which this limit is exceeded until the allowance is fully abated.

This means that anyone with income of more than £118,880 loses all their personal allowance.

However, it is possible to preserve entitlement to the personal allowance by reducing income to below £100,000. There are various ways in which this can be achieved, for example by transferring income producing assets to a spouse or civil partner where his or her income is below the £100,000 abatement limit.

Likewise, adjusted net income can be reduced by making pension contributions, which is in itself beneficial due to the higher rate relief that they receive on contributions up to the available annual allowance. Charitable donations would also work (although the donor would lose the benefit of the donation).

Keeping The Full Personal Allowance

John has adjusted net income of £120,000 for 2013/14, of which £30,000 is in the form of interest from investments. His wife has income of £10,000 for the year.

As John has income in excess of £118,880, he will lose the personal allowance for 2013/14. By transferring the investments to his wife, his income is reduced to £90,000 and he retains the personal allowance.

For a higher rate taxpayer paying tax at 40% the personal allowance is worth £3,776 for 2013/14 (£9,440 @ £40%). By transferring income to his wife John retains the personal allowance, saving £3,776. As the income transferred to his wife is taxed at 20% rather than at 40%, the couple save a further £6,000 in tax (see Tip 6).

3.   Age-Related Tax Allowances

People born before 6 April 1948 receive higher personal allowances. In a measure dubbed as the 'granny tax' the age-related element of the personal allowance is being gradually phased out. The allowances, previously available for persons aged 65 and over with a higher allowance for those aged 75 and over are now only available to persons born before 6 April 1948, with a higher allowance for those born before 6 April 1938. The age-related allowances are to remain frozen at the 2012/13 levels until the basic personal allowance catches up, at which point they will be abolished.

For 2013/14 the personal allowance for people born on or after 6 April 1938 and before 6 April 1948 is set at £10,500 and the personal allowance for those born before 6 April 1938 is set at £10,660. The age-related element is abated if income exceeds the income threshold, which is set at £26,100 for 2013/14. The basic personal allowance is set at £9,440 for 2013/14.

To ensure that the age-related element is not lost unnecessarily, care should be taken to ensure income producing assets are held in the most tax-efficient manner to preserve entitlement to the higher age-related allowances where possible. This may mean transferring assets between spouses/civil partners to keep income of one partner below the abatement limit. Where only one partner is entitled to the age-related allowance, the aim is to keep that partner's income below the abatement limit and where both partners have age-related allowances, if one is entitled to the higher allowance (if born before 6 April 1938), his or her income should, if possible, be kept below the abatement limit.

Age-Related Tax Allowances

Mr Smith was born in July 1939 and his wife in May 1940.

Mr Smith has income of £40,000, and Mrs Smith has no income whatsoever.

In this situation, Mr Smith would be entitled to the age-related allowance for 2013/14 for persons born on or after 6 April 1938 and before 6 April 1948 of £10,500. Mrs Smith is also entitled to the allowance, but as she has no income her allowance would be wasted.

As Mr Smith has income in excess of £26,100, the age-related portion of his allowance would be fully abated such that he receives the standard personal allowance for 2013/14 of £9,440.

By redistributing the income producing assets so that for 2013/14 they both have income of at least £10,500 but below £26,100 Mr and Mrs Smith could gain full use of their age-related allowance.

By doing this they will benefit from combined personal allowances of £21,000 as compared to £9,440 prior to the income redistribution. This will save tax for 2013/14 of £2,312 ((£21,000 - £9,440) x 20%).

4. Utilising Your Annual CGT Exemption

If you have significant capital gains within your portfolio then it is important to utilise the annual capital gains tax exempt amount.

For the 2013/14 tax year this is worth £10,900 per person, and is one of the most generous annual allowances in the world.

Any disposals within this figure are exempt from capital gains tax.

This means that you can use your tax-free allowance each year by selling off just enough shares (or other qualifying assets) to realise a gain equivalent to the annual exemption.

Utilising this exemption could also significantly boost your overall return over a number of years.

Please note that this allowance cannot be carried forward. So this means that if it is not used in the tax year then it is lost!

To view the allowances for previous years please use this link: http://www.hmrc.gov.uk/rates/cgt.htm.

Using Your Annual CGT Allowance

Smart John

John has a significant share portfolio and is a higher rate taxpayer.

For 2013/14 he will be liable to capital gains tax at 28% on any gains in excess of his capital gains tax annual exempt amount.

He has held these shares for a number of years, and has always made use of his annual exemption for capital gains tax purposes, selling sufficient shares to realise a gain approximately equal to the capital gains tax exempt amount (£10,900 for 2013/14).

By utilising his annual exemption for 2013/14 he is able to realise tax-free gains of £10,900 thereby saving capital gains tax of £3,052 (£10,900 @ 28%).

This means that as a result of using his annual exemption each year and only making disposals within the annual exemption rather than disposing of his shares all in one go, he is much better off as any gains on the shares are realised tax-free.

Not So Smart Jack

Jack does not spread the sale of his shares over several years but instead sells shares and realises gains of £25,000 in 2013/14.

He has other income of £50,000.

As he is a higher rate taxpayer, he pays capital gains tax at 28%.

The annual exemption of £10,900 is set against the gain of £25,000, leaving net chargeable gains of £14,100. He pays tax on these gains of £3,948 (£14,100 @ 28%), leaving him with £21,052 after tax to reinvest.

Compare this with John, who realised his gains completely tax-free by selling his shares over a number of years and making best use of the annual allowance.

5. Utilising Spouse's Or Civil Partner's Annual CGT Exemption

Each spouse or civil partner has their own capital gains tax annual exempt amount. Further, assets can be transferred between spouses and civil partners at a value that gives neither a gain nor a loss. By transferring assets into joint names prior to sale or to your spouse or civil partner, you can utilise your spouse's or civil partner's annual capital gains tax exempt amount as well as your own if he or she has not used it.

For 2013/14 the annual exemption is £10,900 which means that a couple can make gains of up to £21,800 before paying any capital gains tax.

Transfers between spouses and civil partners are treated as a no gain/no loss transaction and hence the spouse/civil partner steps into the shoes of the other holder, taking over their base cost and length of ownership.

This can be especially useful when selling investment properties, although stamp duty land tax considerations need to be taken into account.

Utilising Spouse's/Civil Partner's CGT Allowance

Mr Smith (a higher rate taxpayer) wants to sell shares in 2013/14 which will realise a taxable gain of £21,000.

If he goes ahead and sells the shares and utilises his annual exemption, he will pay capital gains tax on £10,100 @ 28% = £2,828.

However, if Mr Smith transfers half of the shares to his wife prior to the sale then Mr and Mrs Smith would each have a taxable gain of £10,500, which would be covered by their annual exemption of £10,900.

By using their annual exemptions (£10,900 each) the shares can be sold without triggering a capital gains tax liability leaving them £2,828 better off.

6.   Equalising Marginal Rates Of Tax

For 2013/14 there are three rates of income tax – the basic rate of 20%, the higher rate of 40% and the additional rate of 45%.

By transferring income to a lower earning spouse or civil partner it is possible to save tax at the higher rates, thereby reducing the combined tax bill.

It should be noted that to transfer income to a spouse or civil partner, the underlying asset, such as shares, must be transferred, rather than the income (for example, the dividend) itself.

Equalising Marginal Rates Of Tax

Stuart is an additional rate taxpayer with income of £170,000. His wife has income of £50,000 (after deducting personal allowances).

By transferring income of £20,000 to his wife, the marginal rate of tax is reduced from 45% to 40%, saving tax of £1,000 (5% of £20,000).

A word of caution: where it is not possible to reduce income below £100,000 for both partners to preserve personal allowances, care should be taken to avoid the high marginal rates that occur between the income limit and the level at which the personal allowance is fully abated (for 2013/14 between £100,000 and £118,880).

If Stuart's wife had been a basic rate taxpayer, it is possible to generate greater savings and in this situation it is advisable to transfer sufficient income to use the whole of her basic rate band. The basic rate band is set at £32,010 for 2013/14 and the personal allowance is £9,440 making it possible to have income of £41,450 before paying higher rate tax.

Chapter 2.
Savings and Investments

7.   Individual Savings Accounts

Use your Individual Savings Account (ISA) allowance each year to enjoy tax-free interest.

For 2013/14 the limit is £11,520 (of which up to £5,760 can be invested in cash).

You can invest in cash, insurance, stocks and shares, etc. up to the limit each year and all proceeds are free from personal taxation. Investing at the start of each year maximises the tax-free return.

Using an ISA to invest £10,000 each year for ten years will provide a pot of £100,000 plus accumulated interest which is generating tax-free returns. Over a number of years this can be a viable alternative to a pension fund as proceeds can be taken at any time and there is no requirement to wait for retirement age or to take an annuity.

These ISAs are also useful for the retention of income within the fund as this is received effectively tax-free. This means that the fund can grow at a faster rate than if the funds were held outside an ISA where potentially 20%, 40% or 45% of the investment return would be taxed.

Individual Savings Account

Craig invests £7,000 into shares using his ISA. After three years, this has grown to £14,000, and he decides to cash it in. He has used his annual capital gains tax allowance elsewhere.

The amount of tax he pays on the gain is NIL. However, if he had made the investment outside an ISA, purchasing shares in his own name, he would pay capital gains tax on the gain of £7,000.

If he is a higher rate taxpayer, he would face a capital gains tax bill of £1,960 (£7,000 @ 28%).

8.   Junior ISAs

Use your children's Junior ISA limit.

Junior ISAs are long-term savings accounts for children. A child can have a Junior ISA if he or she is under 18, lives in the UK and does not have a child trust fund account.

The money belongs to the child, although anyone can put money in. There are two types of Junior ISA – cash Junior ISA and a stocks and shares Junior ISA. A child can have one or both.

The maximum amount that can be paid into a Junior ISA is £3,720 for 2013/14. Income and gains are tax-free. Except in very limited circumstances the money cannot be withdrawn until the child is 18. An ISA can be used to build up a nice savings pot for the child or maybe to fund university or college.

Once a child reaches 16, they can open an adult cash ISA and take advantage of the higher investment limits.

Junior ISAs

David invests £3,000 a year for the next 18 years into a Junior ISA for his baby daughter Lucy. When Lucy reaches 18, she will have a fund of £54,000 plus accumulated interest.

The interest is tax-free and is not taxed as David's income.

9.   Bank And Building Society Interest

If you are a non-taxpayer, make sure you register for interest to be paid gross and if you have not done that, make sure that you claim back any tax paid on interest earned on bank and building society deposits.

To receive interest gross you should complete the HMRC form R85.

You can download the form via the following link:

http://www.hmrc.gov.uk/forms/r85.pdf.

If tax has already been deducted this can be reclaimed on form R40. This is available to download via the following link:

http://www.hmrc.gov.uk/forms/r40.pdf.

Bank And Building Society Interest
Henry holds £50,000 on deposit and receives interest of £2,000 net of 20% tax.
He has no other income for the year.
He is therefore entitled to reclaim the £500 tax deducted from his interest by utilising his personal allowance against this income.
Also, in future years he should file form R85 to receive the interest gross.

10.   Children's Bonus Bond

Children's Bonus Bonds are a tax-free investment issued by National Savings.

Children's bonus bonds allow investments to be made in the child's own name and there is no tax to pay on the interest or on any bonuses. The maximum investment is £3,000 per issue (minimum £25 per issue) and the term is a minimum of five years.

This can be a useful product for generating income and a nest egg for your children and is not affected by the rules concerning income generated by gifts from parents for children.

For issue 35, each £25 unit earns an interest rate of 2.50% AER including the five-year bonus.

Children's Bonus Bond

Freddy invests £3,000 into an issue 35 Children's Bonus Bond to be held for the benefit of his one-year-old daughter Kelly. The bond earns interest at a rate of 2.50% AER guaranteed over five years.

After five years the bond is worth £3,394.22. Freddy has earned tax-free income for his daughter of £394.22.

11. The 10% Savings Rate Of Tax

Savings income is charged to tax at a rate of 10% up to the savings rate limit of £2,790 (2013/14 figures). The savings rate only applies if taxable non-savings income does not exceed the savings rate limit.

If you have savings income that qualifies for the savings rate and that income has suffered a tax deduction at source of 20% (for example bank interest paid net), you can reclaim the difference between the tax deducted (20%) and the tax due at the savings rate (10%) on form R40. You can download the form via the following link: http://www.hmrc.gov.uk/forms/r40.pdf.

The 10% Savings Rate Of Tax

Simon receives bank interest of £9,500 (net). The interest has suffered deduction of tax at the basic rate of 20%. This is Simon's only income.

Simon's gross savings income is £11,875 (£9,500 x 100/80). He is entitled to the personal allowance of £9,440 for 2013/14. His taxable savings income is therefore £2,435. As this is less than the savings rate limit for 2013/14 of £2,790, Simon pays tax at the savings rate of 10%.

The tax due on Simon's savings is therefore £243.50 (£2,435 @ 10%). He has suffered tax at source of £2,375.

He can therefore reclaim £2,135.50 on form R40. The claim extends not only to the savings income covered by his personal allowance (£1,888 being £9,440 @20%), but also repayment of half the tax suffered at source on his taxable savings income of £2,435 (£243.50), which is liable to tax at 10% rather than the 20% deducted.

12.   Using The Savings Rate: Couples

For 2013/14 the first £2,790 of taxable savings income is taxed at a special rate of 10%. Thereafter, savings income is taxed at 20%. The special savings rate is not available if the taxpayer has taxable non-savings income of more than £2,790.

By moving interest-earning accounts between spouses and partners it is possible to take advantage of the special rate for savings and to save tax on savings income.

Using The Savings Rate: Couples

Alfred and Freda are both retired. Alfred has a pension of £20,000 a year. He has also accumulated savings over the years which generate interest of £2,500 a year.

Freda has a pension of £10,500 a year.

Both are entitled to the age allowance of £10,500 for 2013/14.

By transferring the savings into Freda's name, they will be able to benefit from the savings rate of 10%, paying tax of £250 on the interest rather than tax of £500 (£2,500 @ 20%).

13. Do You Have Savings And Are Still Paying A Mortgage?

If the interest rate on your mortgage is higher than the interest you earn on your savings, then you can save a considerable amount of money and reduce your tax bill on interest received by using spare capital to pay off the mortgage on your own property. In the current climate of low interest rates where savings earn a very poor rate of return this is likely to be worthwhile.

You could also save considerable tax by switching to an offset mortgage if you feel the need to have the capital easily available should the need for it arise.

Remember that your mortgage payments are made from your after-tax income and hence cost you a lot more in total income to fund than you may think.

Savings And Mortgages

John has £30,000 earning 2% per annum in interest, which equates to 1.2% net of higher rate tax at 40%. He also has a mortgage of £30,000 on which he pays interest at a rate of 3.5%. This costs him £1,050 a year, which is payable from his after-tax income.

By paying off the mortgage, he no longer pays the £1,050 in interest per annum on this and also no longer receives the £360 in interest the money earned him after tax. He is therefore £690 a year better off.

Funding the mortgage payments was costing John £1,750 in gross income, which he could now use for other purposes, e.g. to increase his pension funding, which would save him further tax.

14. Dividends And Non-Taxpayers

Dividends are received with a non-refundable 10% tax credit.

Because this cannot be reclaimed by non-taxpayers, it is worthwhile considering changing investments so as to receive savings income, such as bank or building society interest, rather than dividends.

This is because bank and building society interest suffers a 20% tax deduction, which can be claimed back by a non-taxpayer.

Non-taxpayers can also register to receive bank and building society interest gross (see Tip 9). The ability to receive the full amount of savings income can be very important for pensioners on low incomes relying on their investments to generate income in retirement.

Dividends And Non-Taxpayers

Mr and Mrs Smith have built up a portfolio of investments, which currently yield £9,900 (gross) per annum in dividends. The dividends are all received with a 10% tax credit, which leaves a net income of £8,910. They have no other income.

By switching their investment strategy Mr and Mrs Smith (say by investing in Government Stock), and assuming they receive the same gross income of £9,900 with a 20% tax deduction. This leaves them with a net income of £7,920.

By filing tax repayment claims and utilising their personal allowances, they receive back the £1,980 tax deducted and are left with a net income of £9,900.

This means that they are better off by £990 (or 10%).

This can be a very significant amount of money, especially for those on low incomes.

A word of caution. When making investment decisions you should consider the return on investment and any costs, as well as the tax savings, and ensure that the net result from making the switch is beneficial.

15.   Pension Funding

Payments into an approved pension scheme attract tax relief at your highest rate of tax and are deemed to be paid net of basic rate tax.

From 2013/14 the annual limit on tax-relieved pension savings is set at £50,000. Relief for contributions up to the limit is given at the taxpayer's marginal rate of tax, meaning that pension contributions are tax-effective, especially for higher and additional rate taxpayers.

It is also possible to carry forward unused allowances from the previous three tax years (subject to a cap of £50,000 per year on tax-relieved pension savings where allowances are brought forward for years before 2011/12), which means that it is possible to make significant tax-relieved contributions to a registered pension scheme.

The annual allowance is to be reduced to £40,000 from 2014/15.

A basic rate taxpayer will effectively pay £80 for a £100 contribution into a registered pension scheme. For higher rate taxpayers, a £100 pension contribution costs £60 and for additional rate taxpayers, the cost is just £55. This makes pension savings particularly tax-efficient.

Pension Funding

John invests £2,000 into his pension scheme, which costs him £1,600 as this is paid net of basic rate tax, which the pension fund recovers bringing the pension contribution to £2,000.

As a higher rate taxpayer paying tax at 40% he claims higher rate tax relief on this and receives a tax rebate of £400 (being the difference between the higher rate relief due of £800 and the basic rate relief already given of £400 (i.e. 20% of £2,000)) from HMRC.

Jack is an additional rate taxpayer paying tax at 45%. He too invests £2,000 into his pension scheme, which costs him £1,600 as this is paid net of basic rate tax.

As an additional rate taxpayer he can claim further tax relief of £500 from HMRC, which he receives as a tax rebate. This is 25% of £2,000, being the difference between the basic rate (20%) and the additional rate of 45%.

16.   Making The Most Of The £50,000 Pension Tax Annual Allowance

Tax relief on pension contributions is available on contributions up to the annual allowance. To the extent it is unused the annual allowance can be carried forward for up to three years.

This means that where a member of a registered pension scheme has not made any contributions in the previous three years it is possible to make tax-relieved contributions of up to £200,000 (earnings permitting) in 2013/14.

The annual allowance will fall to £40,000 from 2014/15, reducing the extent to which it is possible to make tax-relieved pension contributions and the degree to which pension contributions can be used as a planning tool, for example to reduce income and preserve entitlement to the personal allowance for those with income in excess of £100,000.

Making The Most Of The £50,000 Pension Annual Allowance

Paul is an additional rate taxpayer. He makes contributions into his pension scheme up to the level of the annual allowance each year to take advantage of the tax relief available.

In 2013/14 he makes a contribution of £50,000. He pays it net of basic rate tax, making a payment of £40,000 and receives tax relief of £10,000 at source.

As he is an additional rate taxpayer, he claims further tax relief of £12,500 via his self-assessment tax return (being the difference between additional rate relief of 45% on the contribution of £50,000 and the basic rate relief of 20% given at source). In total, he receives tax relief of £22,500 and the contribution to his pension scheme costs him £27,500.

In 2014/15 the annual allowance is reduced to £40,000. Paul makes contributions up to this limit. He will receive tax relief of £18,000 (compared to £22,500 in 2013/14) and his contribution of £40,000 will cost him £22,000.

Making contributions up to the annual allowance allows Paul to take advantage of the tax relief on offer.

17. Making Pension Contributions For Family Members

Most people are unaware that the Government allows contributions of up to £3,600 gross (£2,880 net of basic rate tax) to be made into a registered pension scheme regardless of your level of income or age.

So if you want you can contribute into a pension scheme for your non-working spouse, children, etc., and they are deemed to have made the contribution net of basic rate tax even if they are non-taxpayers.

Making Pension Contributions For Family Members

John wishes to increase his family's pension fund at retirement and makes a contribution of £2,880 into his non-working wife's pension fund.

This is worth £3,600 in the scheme and he is able to obtain a tax saving of £720 by doing so.

He also contributes £2,880 into each of his three children's pension schemes which again is worth £3,600 in each of their schemes, receiving a further £720 tax advantage in each scheme (£2,160 in total).

As the children will have their pension scheme running for much longer than someone who does not start a pension until they start work, they will have a considerably bigger pension fund at retirement than, say, someone starting their pension funding at the typical age of 30.

18. Invest In A Venture Capital Trust (VCT)

If your attitude to investment risk is at the higher end of the scale then you could invest in a Venture Capital Trust (VCT). These are designed to encourage investment into smaller higher-risk trading companies.

These have significant tax benefits as they allow you to reduce capital gains tax liabilities and attract income tax relief at 30% on your investment.

The first two of the following benefits apply to shares which were acquired in a tax year in which no more than £200,000 VCT shares were acquired.

Three significant benefits of investing money into a VCT are:

- No capital gains tax is paid when the shares are sold,
- Dividends are received tax-free, and
- No CGT is payable within the trust.

Invest In A Venture Capital Trust

John invests £10,000 into a VCT.

He receives a £3,000 tax rebate after submitting his Tax Return, which is the equivalent of 30% of his investment.

19. Invest In An Enterprise Investment Scheme (EIS)

EIS schemes offer tax relief on contributions at 30% and a tax deferral on gains. EIS investments are generally high risk and invest in a single company.

If the investment is into your own company, only CGT deferral relief is available.

Investing In An EIS

John and EIS

John decides to set up a new trading business and subscribes for £50,000 of shares at par, and has gains realised elsewhere of £50,000 which he invests in the shares.

The company qualifies for EIS treatment and he applies for an EIS scheme number. He elects to defer the gains into the new shares, and saves having to pay capital gains tax on his gains.

This gives him a capital gains tax deferral of £14,000 (28% of £50,000)!

Alisha and EIS

Alisha invests £50,000 into a qualifying EIS company in 2013/14 with which she has no connection.

She has gains of £50,000 for the year that she invests in the EIS. She defers the £14,000 tax payable on her gains, and also receives a tax rebate of 30% of her contribution, i.e. £15,000.

20. Re-Invest Gains In A Seed Enterprise Investment Scheme (SEIS)

The Seed Enterprise Investment Scheme (SEIS) was introduced in 2012 to help small, early-stage companies to raise equity finance by offering tax reliefs to investors who purchase new shares in a company within the scheme.

To kick-start investment CGT relief was given in 2012/13 on chargeable gains reinvested in shares qualifying for SEIS relief. Re-invested gains are exempt from CGT, subject to the £100,000 investment limit.

This relief has been extended and is available in respect of gains realised in 2013/14 which are reinvested in SEIS shares. The re-investment must take place in 2013/14 or 2014/15 and relief from capital gains tax is available for half of the amount re-invested (subject to the £100,000 investment limit).

Re-Invest Gains In A Seed Enterprise Investment Scheme (SEIS)

Toby realises gains of £100,000 in 2013/14 which he re-invests in shares in a SEIS scheme. The investment is made in 2013/14.

Toby is an additional rate taxpayer and has utilised his capital gains tax annual exempt amount elsewhere.

He receives capital gains tax relief on 50% of the amount reinvested (£50,000), on which he saves capital gains tax of £14,000 (£50,000 @ 28%).

Chapter 3.
Family Companies

21. Pay A Small Salary To Retain State Pension

Where a person's earnings fall between the lower earnings limit for Class 1 National Insurance purposes (£109 per week for 2013/14) and the primary earnings threshold (£149 per week for 2013/14) they are deemed to have paid National Insurance Contributions at a notional zero rate.

The benefit of this is that it preserves their contribution record and entitlement to the state pension and certain contributory benefits, without actually costing them anything.

Therefore, where profits are extracted in the form of dividends, it is beneficial to also pay a small salary.

For 2013/14, a salary of between £5,688 and £7,696 per annum (£473 and £641 per month) can be paid without triggering a liability to either employee or employer Class 1 National Insurance contributions.

As a salary at this level is below the PAYE threshold, no PAYE tax needs to be paid. However, the employer must report pay details to HMRC under real time information.

22.   Efficient Extraction Of Profits

There are various ways in which profits can extracted from a personal or family company and consideration should be given to formulating a tax-efficient extraction policy. As circumstances vary there is no substitute for crunching the numbers and it is advisable to take professional advice.

A popular and effective strategy is to pay a small salary of above the lower earnings limit (£109 per week for 2013/14) and below the secondary threshold for National Insurance purposes (£148 per week for 2013/14). This will preserve entitlement to the state pension and contributory benefits (see Tip 21) but can be paid free of tax and National Insurance. Thereafter, profits should be extracted as dividends as long as the company has sufficient retained profits. This is generally more tax efficient than paying a salary or bonus as no National Insurance contributions are due on dividends. Also, no further tax is payable on dividend income until the basic rate limit is reached.

Dividends are paid from after-tax profits and must be properly declared in accordance with company law.

Salary payments and employer's NIC are deductible in computing profits for corporation tax purposes.

Efficient Extraction Of Profits

Olly is the sole shareholder and director of OB Ltd.

He pays himself a salary of £8,000 a year and has other income of £3,000 a year.

He has profits before tax of £20,000 which he wants to withdraw as a salary or a dividend.

If he pays a salary, no corporation tax will be due. He has £20,000 available to cover the salary and employer's NIC. He can pay himself a salary of £17,575 (£20,000 x 100/113.8) on which employer's NIC of £2,425 is due.

He must pay tax at 20% on the salary (£3,515) and employee NIC at 12% (£2,109).

He therefore retains profits of £11,951.

If he takes the dividend route, corporation tax of 20% is payable on the profits, leaving retained profits of £16,000 for distribution.

Dividends are paid net of a 10% tax credit so Olly is treated as receiving a gross dividend of £17,777 on which tax of 10% (£1,777 – fully matched by the tax credit) is due.

By taking the dividend route rather than the salary route, Olly is able to retain £16,000 of the profits rather than £11,591, leaving him £4,409 better off.

23. Dividends Below The Higher Rate Threshold

If you do not need the income or wish to build up funds within the company, restricting dividends paid to just below the higher rate threshold can save considerable amounts of tax.

Dividends Below The Higher Rate Threshold

John does not need more than £30,000 per annum to live on so pays dividends just below the higher rate threshold (£41,450 for 2013/14). He has no other income.

A gross dividend of £41,450 equates to a net dividend of £37,305. As dividends must be paid out of after-tax profits, John will need profits of £46,631 (on which corporation tax of £9,326 must be paid) to pay a net dividend of £37,305.

By doing this, John does not need to pay any tax on the dividends as the liability to tax at the dividend ordinary rate of 10% is matched by the associated tax credit.

24. Fluctuating Dividends

By fluctuating the payment of dividends so as to pay a large dividend one year and a small dividend the following year, it is possible to avoid having to make payments on account, which achieves a cash-flow advantage by delaying the date on which tax is due.

Fluctuating Dividends

John is a higher rate taxpayer, and aims to draw out £50,000 per annum on average in (gross) dividends from his company.

By fluctuating the amount of dividends and only drawing out sufficient dividends to take advantage of the basic rate tax band in alternate years, he can avoid paying payments on account and hence achieve a cash-flow advantage.

Assume he withdrew £42,475 (gross) in dividends in 2012/13 and this was his only income.

As there is no tax to pay for 2012/13 payments, on account are not due for 2013/14.

If he pays dividends of £57,525 in 2013/14, the higher rate liability will not be due until 31 January 2015 (rather than in equal instalments on 31 January 2014 and 31 July 2014 which would have been the case had he paid dividends of £50,000 in each tax year).

---

25. Timing Of Bonus Payments To Delay Tax

Due to the way the tax rules work, it is possible to have a deduction for a bonus declared in a set of company accounts and pay this up to nine months after the year-end.

This could be in a different tax year where other income is lower and this would result in a lower tax liability. Alternatively a deferral of the timing of the tax payment could be made.

Timing Of Bonus Payments

Jane is preparing the company accounts for XYZ Ltd, her own limited company.

The company's year-end is 31 December 2012. She declares a bonus for the year to 31 December 2012 and makes provision in the accounts. The bonus is due for payment and actually paid in August 2013.

As the bonus is paid within nine months of the company year-end, a deduction is permitted for corporation tax purposes in the company accounts for the year to 31 December 2012. However, the bonus is taxed for PAYE purposes when it is paid in August 2013.

26. Employ Your Family

If a member of your family has no income, you could employ them in your family business and save a significant amount of tax for the family as a whole.

Care must be taken to ensure that the arrangement is commercial and the level of pay is commensurate with the duties performed to avoid an attack from HMRC.

The National Minimum Wage rules also need to be considered, although the National Minimum Wage does not apply to directors, unless they have a contract of employment.

Employing Your Family

John's wife Kelly has no income, but spends a considerable amount of time answering the telephone in John's home office and dealing with correspondence.

She also has the task of keeping track of the accounts, for which she is not paid.

By paying her a salary he can reduce his own exposure to higher rate tax and reward her for the efforts she puts in on behalf of the business.

This simple strategy can save several thousand pounds in tax along the way.

27. Considering Disincorporation? Limited Window For Disincorporation Relief

Although reliefs are available to a business that chooses to incorporate, historically there have been no corresponding reliefs for companies that wish to disincorporate, and tax charges can arise where a company wishes to transfer business assets to shareholders who want to carry on the business in an unincorporated form.

To remove barriers to disincorporation, disincorporation relief is available for five years from 6 April 2013. The relief enables assets to be transferred at a reduced value for corporation tax purposes. It is only available to businesses whose qualifying assets do not have a market value in excess of £100,000.

The relief must be claimed jointly by the company and by the shareholders who wish to carry on the business in an unincorporated form.

A word of caution – the relief does not cover tax charges that may arise on shareholders where assets are distributed below market value in the course of a disincorporation.

Chapter 4.

Employers and Employees

28. Quarterly PAYE Payments

For employers, an important cash-flow advantage can be obtained by making PAYE payments quarterly rather than monthly.

This is a choice employers have, provided their payments do not exceed £1,500 per month on average.

Quarterly PAYE Payments

John has one full-time employee, and his total PAYE deductions per month average less than £1,500.

He chooses to pay by quarterly instalments and hence has the use of up to £4,500 for a couple of months.

This can be a very useful payment strategy when money may be tight.

29. Pay PAYE On Time To Avoid Penalties

Penalties are charged if PAYE is paid late on more than one occasion in the tax year.

The penalty charged for late payment is a percentage of the PAYE paid late.

The penalty rate is linked to the number of occasions on which payment was made late in the tax year, ranging from 1% if payment is made late on two, three or four occasions in the year to 4% if payment is made late on 11 or 12 occasions.

A further penalty of 5% is charged if payment is outstanding after six months. If payment remains due after 12 months, a subsequent 5% penalty is levied.

A PAYE month runs to the 5th of each month. Where payment is made electronically, cleared funds must reach HMRC's bank account by the 22nd of the month. Payments of PAYE and NIC must reach HMRC by the 19th of the month if paid by cheque.

But see Tip 30 below where the normal payment date falls on a weekend or bank holiday.

30.　Tips When Making PAYE Payments

As highlighted in Tip 29, PAYE should be paid on time each month to avoid late payment penalties.

However, to avoid getting caught out by bank holidays and weekends, ensure that payment is made early when the normal payment day falls on a bank holiday or a weekend. When this happens, the payment (or in the case of electronic payments, cleared funds) must reach HMRC by the last working day before the bank holiday or weekend on which the normal payment day falls.

In 2013/14, where payment is not made electronically (so must reach HMRC by the 19th of the month), payment should be made early in May 2013, October 2013 and January 2014 to allow for the fact that the 19th falls on a weekend.

Where payment is made electronically, payment should be sent early in June 2013, September 2013, December 2013, February 2014 and March 2014 to allow for the fact that the 22nd falls on a weekend (unless the Faster Payment service is used).

Allow For Bank Holidays And Weekends When Making Payments Of PAYE

Jake pays his PAYE by cheque each month, posting the cheque on the 16th of the month to allow sufficient time for posting. His payment for PAYE month 1 (month to 5 May 2013) must reach HMRC by 19 May 2013.

However, as this falls on a Sunday, in reality it must reach HMRC the previous Friday (17th May).

Jake must therefore post his cheque by 14th May rather than 16th May to ensure it reaches HMRC on time.

If the cheque arrived on Saturday 18th May, it would be treated by HMRC as having been received on Monday 20th May and the payment would be regarded as late.

If Jake then paid late on one more occasion during 2013/14, he would suffer a late payment penalty.

This can be avoided by posting the cheque a few days early when the normal payment date falls on a weekend.

31. Use Basic PAYE Tools

Under real time information (RTI) employers must report details of pay and tax deducted to HMRC electronically at or before the time at which payment is made to the employee. Most employers will migrate to RTI from the start of the 2013/14 tax year and all employers (subject to a few limited exceptions for particular PAYE schemes) must report in real time by October 2013.

To meet their obligations under RTI, employers must use RTI-compliant payroll software. There are numerous software solutions available.

However, employers with nine or fewer employees can use HMRC's free Basic PAYE Tools software package to meet their obligations under RTI without having to spend money on a commercial software package.

Basic PAYE Tools can be downloaded from the HMRC website (see www.hmrc.gov.uk/payerti/payroll/bpt/paye-tools.htm).

32.   Dispensations For Employers

You can save a considerable amount of time and money by applying to HMRC for a dispensation for certain business expenses reimbursed to employees by the company.

A dispensation frees the employer from having to report certain expenses to HMRC and can be granted for those expenses in respect of which a corresponding tax deduction can be claimed.

A dispensation also removes the need for the employee to claim the tax deduction, saving work all round.

This applies to any size of company, from a one-person company to large multi-nationals, although obviously the more employees you have, the more time you will save in not having to complete the sections of the P11D that are no longer relevant once a dispensation has been granted.

Dispensations For Employers

Frank is fed up with the time-consuming job of completing P11Ds for his employees when all he does is reimburse business expenses.

He applies for and is granted a dispensation for the business expenses of his employees.

This means that he no longer has to complete P11Ds for the employees as no benefits are reportable. Therefore it leaves him with more time to get on with running the business.

33.   Claim A Deduction For Mileage Payments

Under the Approved Mileage Allowance Payments (AMAP) Scheme employers can pay employees tax-free mileage rates when they use their own car for business. Provided that the amounts paid do not exceed the rates set by HMRC, no tax liability arises and there is nothing to report on the P11D.

However, many employees are unaware that if their employer pays them at a rate that is less than the approved rate they can claim a tax deduction for the shortfall. The approved rates for 2013/14 for cars and vans are 45p per mile for the first 10,000 business miles in the tax year and 25p thereafter.

Claim A Deduction For Mileage Allowances

Nigel uses his own car for work and in 2013/14 undertakes 9,000 business miles. His employer pays a mileage allowance of 30p per mile. Thus, Nigel receives mileage allowances of £2,700 during the year.

However, at the approved rate of 45p per mile for the first 10,000 business miles, John's employer could pay him a tax-free allowance of £4,050 (9,000 miles @ 45p per mile). This is known as 'the approved amount'.

Nigel can claim a tax deduction of £1,350 for the shortfall between the approved amount (£4,050) and the amount he is actually paid (£2,700). Assuming Nigel is a higher rate taxpayer paying tax at 40%, this will save him tax of £540.

34. Company Cars – The CO_2 Rating

Because the car benefit charge and fuel scale charge are linked to the carbon dioxide emissions from the car, consider changing to a lower emission car and you can save considerable amounts in tax.

For more detailed information and the tax rates please use the following link www.hmrc.gov.uk/cars/index.htm to view the guidance on the HMRC website.

Company Cars – The CO_2 Rating

Bill is a higher rate taxpayer and pays tax at 40%. He works for ABC Ltd. He has a company car, which is available for private use.

By switching from a car with an emission rating of 210 g/km to one with a rating of 135 g/km, the taxable benefit on a £20,000 list price car changes from £6,800 (34% of £20,000) to £3,800 (19% of £20,000) (2013/14 figures).

The reduction in the benefit reduces the tax payable from £2,720 (£6,800 @ 40%) to £1,520 (£3,800 @ 40%) and saves tax of £1,200. The employer would also save Class 1A National Insurance Contributions of £414.

If fuel is also provided, the fuel benefit would be reduced from £7,174 (34% of £21,100) to £4,009 (19% of £21,100), reducing the tax payable on the car fuel from £2,869.60 (£7,174 @ 40%) to £1,603.60 (£4,009 @ 40%), saving further tax of £1,266. The employer would also save Class 1A National Insurance Contributions of £436.77.

By choosing a car with actual CO_2 emissions of less than 75 g/km, the percentage of the list price taxed falls to 5%.

35.   Company Cars – Tax-Free Electric Cars

By choosing an electric car it is possible to have a company car tax-free as zero-emission cars have a zero charge for five years from 2010/11.

However, the charge on zero-emissions cars is due to increase to 5% in 2015/16 and to 7% in 2016/17, so the opportunity for a tax-free electric company car is for a limited period only.

Company Cars – Tax-Free Electric Cars

Mark is a higher rate taxpayer.

By choosing an electric car that has zero emissions he is able to enjoy the benefit of a company car tax free up to and including 2014/15. This can generate considerable savings.

For example, if instead he chose a car costing £30,000 with CO_2 emissions of 195g/km, for 2013/14 he would be taxed on 31% of the list price, i.e. £9,300. At 40%, the tax payable would be £3,720.

Choosing an electric car can generate significant tax savings.

36.   Cutting Your Fuel Benefit Scale Charge

The fuel benefit charge is very expensive and it may be the case that you can pay more tax on the fuel than on the company car. This will be the case where the list price of the car is less than the fuel multiplier (£21,100 for 2013/14). You may also find that you pay more in tax for the benefit of private fuel than you would spend on fuel for private mileage. It is therefore worthwhile to cut the fuel benefit charge.

There are various ways to do this:

- Buy a new company car with a lower emissions rating as this will reduce the appropriate percentage and consequently the fuel benefit charge.

- Reimburse the company for every drop used privately as this will reduce the fuel scale charge to nil. Eliminating the benefit eliminates the associated tax charge. To make this work, the employee needs to be required to reimburse the full cost of all private fuel and must actually do so. If your private mileage is low, this can be a valuable tax saving for both you and the company. Reimbursement can be made using actual costs or HMRC advisory fuel rates. This is because the current multiplier of £21,100 (2013/14 rate) used in calculating the fuel benefit means that the fuel benefit is often not worthwhile despite high pump prices. It can be cheaper to pay for the fuel than to pay the tax on the benefit.

  Further, the company saves Class 1A NIC at 13.8% on the value of the benefit.

37.   Company Car Or Car Allowance?

Company cars are highly taxed and the tax burden is due to increase in future years as emissions criteria are made stricter, raising the appropriate percentage. Therefore, you should consider whether it would be more appropriate to use your own vehicle for company business.

If you decide to do this then you can claim a car allowance and mileage rate for business miles. Depending on miles covered and the type of car, this can save a considerable amount of tax.

It also has the advantage that if you move jobs you don't have to hand the car back.

Company Car Or Car Allowance?

Bill is an employee. He has a company car with a cash equivalent value of £9,500. He pays tax at 40%. The tax cost of having a company car is £3,800 (£9,500 @ 40%).

He travels 10,000 miles per annum on business, and the company offers him a car allowance of £6,000 per annum instead of his company car. He will pay tax of £2,400 on the allowance and National Insurance of £120.

He will need to fund a car.

When he uses the car for business, Bill is able to claim a tax-free mileage allowance. The allowance is paid at the tax-free rate of 45p per mile for the first 10,000 miles, a total tax-free allowance £4,500 (10,000 miles at 45p per mile).

Bill will be better off in cash terms as he will save the tax on the company car and will receive the car allowance and mileage allowance. If this exceeds the cost of running his own car, he is better off by taking the allowance than taking the company car.

38. Putting Your Mobile Phone Through The Company

An employee can be provided with a mobile phone tax free. This can amount to a valuable tax-free benefit.

However, the exemption only applies if the contract for the provision of the phone is between the mobile phone provider and the company.

This is important.

If the contract is between the employee and the mobile phone provider and the employer pays the bill on the employee's behalf, the employer is regarded as settling a personal liability on the employee's behalf and this must be returned on the P11D and will be taxable as a result.

Even better, HMRC now accept that smartphones fall within the scope of the exemption.

For the use of salary sacrifice arrangements to provide tax-free benefits, see Tip 39.

> **Putting Your Mobile Phone Through The Company**
>
> James' employer provides him with a mobile phone. The contract is between the employer and the mobile phone company and costs the employer £35 per month (£420 a year). This is a tax-free benefit in James' hands.
>
> There is no benefit-in-kind charge on the phone.
>
> If James had met the cost of the phone himself, he would have spent £420 out of his after-tax (and NIC) income.

39. Using Salary Sacrifice Arrangements To Provide Tax-Free Benefits

Many benefits, including childcare vouchers up to the exempt limit and mobile phones can be provided free of tax and National Insurance.

While a tax-free benefit is valuable in the hands of the employee (see Tip 36), the employer is left to meet the cost.

By using a salary sacrifice arrangement it is possible for the employer to pass the cost of the benefit to the employee and for the employee to save tax and National Insurance and the employee to save National Insurance.

Under a salary sacrifice arrangement the employee gives up cash salary for a tax and NIC-free benefit. The employee saves the tax and NIC on the salary given up and the employer saves the employer's NIC.

A word of caution – care must be taken to ensure that the salary sacrifice arrangement is effective. The employment contract should reflect the revised arrangements and the employee must not be able to revert back to the higher salary at will.

Using Salary Sacrifice Arrangements To Provide Tax-Free Benefits

As in Tip 38 James' employer wishes to provide James with a mobile phone. However, the employer does not wish to meet the cost of the phone.

James and his employer enter into a salary sacrifice agreement where James agrees to give up £420 of his annual salary in return for the provision of the mobile phone. The phone contract is between the employer and the mobile phone company.

James is a higher rate taxpayer. He saves tax of £168 (£420 @ 40%) and National Insurance of £8.40 (£420 @ 2%) as a result of swapping cash salary for the exempt benefit of a mobile phone – a total saving of £176.40.

James' employer saves employer NIC of £57.96.

A win-win situation.

40. Working Abroad – Tax-Free Trips For Your Family

If you are sent to work abroad for a continuous period of at least 60 days, then your employer can pay for two trips abroad per tax year for your spouse or civil partner and children without any charge to tax on the costs arising on you.

Care should be taken to space the trips out so that only two per tax year are paid for to avoid a benefit-in-kind charge arising.

If necessary, delay or bring forward a trip to ensure good use of this concession.

Tax-Free Trips For Your Family

In January 2013 Daniel is sent by his employer to work in Dubai for six months.

His employer can pay for two trips each tax year for Daniel's wife and children.

Because his work started in January 2013 he could get four trips paid for in 2013 without suffering a taxable benefit.

This is achieved by taking two trips in the 2012/13 tax year (i.e. before 6 April 2013) and two in the 2013/14 tax year (i.e. after 5 April 2013).

41. Check Your P11D Benefits

When you receive your P11D, remember to check the benefits reported on it and query anything that does not appear right with your company straight away.

There can be mistakes made and it always pays to check!

Also, when completing your Tax Return, ensure that you make the appropriate claim on page 2 of the Tax Return for allowable expenses to ensure you do not end up paying too much tax.

Check Your P11D Benefits

Tim has received a P11D for a number of years and has entered the figures supplied on the form onto page 1 of his employment pages, as instructed by the P11D itself.

He now appoints an adviser, and discovers that he has overpaid several hundred pounds per year in tax as he did not complete page 2 of the employment section claiming the relevant allowable expenses.

His adviser duly helps him submit an appropriate claim and he recovers over £1,000 in overpaid tax.

42. Claiming Expenses If You Don't Fill In A Tax Return

If you do not fill in a Tax Return you need to claim relief for expenses incurred in relation to your employment on form P87. If you do not claim the relief, you will miss out. A claim for 2013/14 must be made by 5 April 2018.

Form P87 is available to download from the HMRC website at www.hmrc.gov.uk/forms/P87.pdf.

Claiming Relief For Expenses If You Don't Fill In A Tax Return

Chris is an employee. Each year he pays professional fees and subscriptions of £700 relevant to his job.

The subscriptions are payable to a body on HMRC's approved list. Chris does not receive any other benefit and does not need to submit a Tax Return.

He claims tax relief for the professional subscriptions on form P87.

The relief is worth £140 to a basic rate taxpayer and £280 to a 40% taxpayer. Had Chris not claimed the relief, he would have missed out.

Chapter 5.
Self-Employed

43. Remember To Tell HMRC That You Are Self-Employed

When you start self-employment you need to tell HMRC as soon as possible. If you do not tell them, you may be charged a penalty.

You can register as self-employed online on the HMRC website (see https://online.hmrc.gov.uk/registration/options. You will be asked questions about your business as part of the registration process. You need to register for self-employment even if you already complete a self-assessment tax return.

You need to register by 5 October after the end of the tax year in which your self-employment started. Penalties may be charged if you fail to register with HMRC.

You will also need to arrange to pay Class 2 NICs (£2.70 per week for 2013/14). You can arrange to pay by direct debit by completing form CA5601 (see www.hmrc.gov.uk/pdfs/ca5601.pdf).

Remember To Tell HMRC That You Are Self-Employed

Polly starts her self-employment making cupcakes in January 2013. She must register with HMRC by 5 October 2013 and must also arrange to pay Class 2 NICs.

If she fails to tell HMRC about her self-employment, she may be charged a penalty.

44. Small Earnings Exception For Class 2 NIC

If you earn less than £5,725 (2013/14 figures) a year from your self-employment you are entitled to claim the small earnings exception and not pay any Class 2 NIC for the year.

At £2.70 a week this is a yearly saving of £140.40 in National Insurance.

Remember that you can also claim this for any year in which you have a loss.

However, if you have no other earnings and are not entitled to NIC credits, you may wish to pay Class 2 contributions voluntarily to preserve entitlement to the state pension.

Small Earnings Exception For Class 2 NIC
Mark has a small self-employment business as well as his full-time employment.
He earns £20,000 in his employment and £4,000 from his self-employment.
Because his self-employment earnings are below the small earnings exception limit for Class 2 NIC, he can claim exemption and save himself Class 2 contributions of £2.70 a week (2013/14 figures).

45.   Choosing Your Accounting Date

When commencing self-employment, choosing an accounting date (the choice of year-end) can be crucial in determining whether low profits are taxed twice or high profits are taxed twice.

It will also determine the level of overlap relief carried forward and utilised on a future change of date or on cessation.

When determining an accounting date, it may be considered easiest if accounts are made up to 31 March or 5 April in the first tax year so as to eliminate any chance of an overlap profit and to maximise the period between the year-end date and the filing deadline for the Tax Return for the year.

Choosing Your Accounting Date

William starts self-employment on 1 May 2012.

He decides on a first accounting date of 30 April 2013 and annually on 30 April thereafter, as his first year is likely to create a small profit whereas he anticipates higher profits thereafter.

He will be taxed on the profits for the period 1 May 2012 to 5 April 2013 twice, as they form the basis of the 2012/13 assessment (1 May 2012 to 5 April 2013) and also part of the 2013/14 assessment (year to 30 April 2013). If his profits are very low, then this could be of a considerable tax benefit to him as he will pay lower taxes than if he chose a 31 March year-end.

However, it should also be noted that his overlap relief going forward will also be correspondingly low and this could cause a problem on cessation (see Tip 48).

46. Use The Cash Basis To Calculate Taxable Income And Save Work

Taxable profits are normally calculated in accordance with Generally Accepted Accounting Practice. This means that profits are determined on the accruals basis by reference to the amount earned in the year, rather than by reference to cash received and paid out.

However, from the 2013/14 tax year small eligible businesses can elect to use the simpler cash basis to work out taxable profits. An election applies for the tax year for which it is made and for subsequent tax years.

The cash basis option is only available to the self-employed and to individuals in partnership whose receipts are not more than the VAT threshold (£79,000 from 1 April 2013). The threshold is doubled where the claimant receives universal credit.

47. Claim Fixed Rate Deductions

To save the work incurred in keeping details of expenses, individuals carrying on a trade as a self-employed sole trader or in partnership with other individuals can instead claim fixed rate deductions.

Fixed rate deductions are available in respect of vehicle deductions, business use of home and in relation to business premises which are also used as a home.

Businesses can choose to claim the fixed rate deductions to save work or can keep records of actual expenditure and make the necessary apportionments between home and business use and claim a deduction for either the actual expense or, where this gives a more favourable result, claim the fixed rate deduction.

Claim Fixed Rate Deductions

Lucy works from home running a small business making soft toys. She works 30 hours a week.

To save paperwork, she claims a fixed rate deduction of £10 per month for use of her home for business purposes.

48.   Choosing A Cessation Date

If your self-employment comes to an end, either naturally or through the decision to incorporate, then be careful as to the date on which you choose to cease trading as this can have a major bearing on the amount of tax payable in the final year.

Choosing A Cessation Date

If William (from Tip 45 case study) chooses to cease on 31 March several years later, as his profits have grown and he is incorporating, then he will be taxed on 23 months' profit in one year with very little in the way of overlap relief.

If, however, he ceases on 1 May in the tax year he will be taxed on the final 12 months of profit only.

This shows that timing the cessation date correctly can save considerable tax.

49. Self-Employed? Then Consider Incorporation

Although the basic rate of income tax at 20% is the same as the small profits rate of corporation tax (20% in financial year 2013), it can still be beneficial to incorporate and extract funds by way of dividends.

This is because dividends do not attract National Insurance Contributions so by incorporating you will save Class 4 National Insurance Contributions.

Self-Employed And Incorporation

Harry incorporates on 6 April 2013, and makes a profit of £50,000 in his first year.

Not only does he now have a choice as to whether to draw this income and pay personal taxes on it or leave it in the company and only incur corporation tax on this, but he also saves a considerable amount by paying himself in dividends rather than a salary as dividends do not attract National Insurance Contributions.

Chapter 6.
Losses

50. Maximising Trading Losses

The use of losses for tax purposes is a complicated topic and many factors come into play.

However, a basic planning tip is to ensure that you are aware of the time limits for making claims and the methods of relief available.

A self-employed person making a trading loss basically has the following options for relieving the loss:

- this year,
- last year (or for accounting periods ending between 24 November 2008 and 23 November 2010, the preceding three years), or
- carry forward against future profits.

The decision as to which way to go will be dependent on a number of factors including:

- future profit levels,
- other income for the year,
- the level of income for the previous year,
- the tax rates in each of those years.

Where a trader opts to use the cash basis (available from 2013/14 where eligibility conditions are met) losses must be carried forward.

Maximising Trading Losses

Raymond has been in business for many years, and makes an allowable trading loss of £30,000 for the accounting period ending 30 June 2013 (which falls in the 2013/14 tax year).

His income is derived purely from his business.

The previous year's profits were £50,000, and he anticipates a profit of £20,000 the following year.

He can carry-back the loss in full to set against the profits of the previous year, recovering some tax at 40% and the balance at 20%.

51. The Loss Relief Extension To Capital Gains

Many people are unaware that if a trading loss is claimed against other income, either for the current or previous year, then by election this can be extended to capital gains, resulting in a further refund of taxes.

This can be of considerable benefit depending on the circumstances.

The Loss Relief Extension

Steve makes a loss in 2012/13 of £50,000.

His income in the same year from other sources is £30,000 and he has chargeable gains (after deducting the annual exemption) of £20,000.

His profit for 2013/14 is likely to be £10,000.

Clearly it is advantageous in this situation to relieve the loss sideways against his other income and extend the claim to cover the capital gains.

Relief is obtained at the earliest opportunity.

52.   Commencement Losses

Unrepresented taxpayers frequently miss out on an additional valuable relief, which is the availability of a three-year carry-back for losses incurred in the opening years of a trade.

Commencement Losses

John was previously employed on a salary of £20,000 per annum, and makes a loss in his first year of trading of £20,000.

He anticipates making a profit the following year of £10,000.

John can elect to carry this loss back three years and hence obtain tax relief on this loss at a higher rate than would otherwise be achieved.

---

53.   Losses On Cessation

A person may decide to stop trading if they are making losses.

Although the loss can be relieved in the usual way against income of the same and previous year, an additional relief is available for the loss made on the cessation of the business (known as a terminal loss).

A claim for terminal loss relief can be made if the person permanently ceases to carry on a trade and makes a terminal loss. The terminal loss is the loss made in the period beginning at the start of the final tax year and ending with the date of cessation plus any loss in the previous 12 months that falls into the previous tax year. The terminal loss may be relieved against the profits of the trade for the final tax year and previous three tax years. Relief is given against a later year before an earlier year.

Alternatively the loss can be set against total income (and extended to capital gains) of the year of the loss and/or the preceding year.

Losses On Cessation

Will has been in business as a sole trader for a number of years. He prepares accounts to 31 March each year. His trade ceases on 30 June 2013.

He makes a profit of £10,000 for the year to 31 March 2013 and a loss of £16,000 for the period from 1 April 2013 to 30 June 2013. He has overlap profits of £5,000 to relieve.

His terminal loss is £13,500 ((9/12 x £10,000) - £16,000 - £5,000).

He makes profits of £9,000 for the year to 31 March 2012 (taxed in 2011/12) and £25,000 for the year to 31 March 2011 (taxed in 2010/11).

He claims terminal loss relief.

The profits for 2012/13 have been taken into account in computing the terminal loss.

The loss is set first against 2011/12 (£9,000) with the remaining £4,500 being set against the profits of 2010/11.

54.   Losses And Capital Allowances

Capital allowances are treated as part of a trading loss for loss relief purposes, and so care should be taken to determine whether disclaiming these and shrinking the loss may actually leave you better off.

This is because personal allowances are ignored in loss claims, so a loss carried back could be wasted if it is set against income that is already covered by personal allowances.

Losses And Capital Allowances

Arthur makes a loss of £30,000 including capital allowances of £5,000.

His taxable profit for the previous tax year was £30,000.

By disclaiming the capital allowances this year he will have more allowances in future years and he preserves the personal allowance in the previous year.

This means that he will save a considerable amount of tax in future years.

Similar logic can be applied in deciding whether to claim the annual investment allowance, or whether this would be wasted and it would be more beneficial to claim the writing down allowance instead.

55. Unlisted Share Losses

Many people subscribe for shares in unlisted companies. These can include companies that your friends own.

A number of these companies will fail and therefore the original investment is lost.

Allowable losses on these shares can be set against income rather than used as a capital loss, which is especially useful if you have no other gains during the year or are unlikely to make capital gains in the future.

Unlisted Share Losses

Louise subscribed for 1,000 shares in ABC Ltd, a company set up by her brother, and paid £10,000 for them. They are now worthless as the company has closed down. She pays tax at 40%.

By claiming income tax relief on this capital loss, she recovers £4,000 of the loss. Had she claimed relief as a capital loss, she would only have recovered £2,800 of the loss.

56. Losses And Tax Credits

If you are self-employed and usually make large profits, but incurred a loss for one year, then you may be eligible to claim working tax credits or universal credit (from October 2013) for that year.

It is worth submitting a protective claim during any year for which you are uncertain of the level of your income as you can only backdate claims for one month from the date of claim.

Losses And Tax Credits

John is married to Mary, who does not work. They have one child age 10.

John usually makes £100,000 per annum as a self-employed consultant.

However, he has just lost his major customer and as a result is likely to make a loss this year, and so submits a claim to working tax credits. It turns out he does make a loss, and is eligible to receive tax credits.

57.   Beware Cap On Income Tax Reliefs

From 6 April 2013 a limit is placed on the amount that an individual may deduct by way of certain specified reliefs. The limit is set at £50,000 or 25% of the individual's adjusted total income for the tax year if this is greater.

The reliefs subject to the limit include income tax loss reliefs, but not charitable donations and contributions to registered pension schemes.

Where reliefs available for the year exceed the limit, care should be taken to ensure that maximum relief is obtained subject to the cap, such as carrying back losses to the previous year or carrying trade losses forward, rather than relieving in the current year. It is advisable that professional advice is sought.

Beware Cap On Income Tax Reliefs

Geoff has income for 2013/14 of £180,000. He makes a trading loss of £60,000. He had no income in 2012/13.

Geoff wishes to set the loss against his general income of 2013/14. However, the relief available for that year is capped at £50,000 as this is greater than 25% of his income (£45,000).

He can claim loss relief of £50,000 for 2013/14. As he had no income in 2012/13, he cannot carry the remainder of the loss back. Therefore he must carry it forward for relief against future profits.

58. Registering Your Capital Losses

If you bought an asset and sold it at a loss then it is possible that you made a capital loss (e.g. if you invested in a start-up that failed or bought an investment property that went down in value, then this may well apply to you).

Capital losses can only be relieved against capital gains and if there are no gains in the year of the loss, the loss can be carried forward. However, if gains are incurred during the year that the loss was made, the loss is first set against the other gains for the year, with any balance remaining unused being carried forward. Losses must be set against gains of the same year before being carried forward, regardless of whether the gains exceed the annual exempt amount for capital gains tax (£10,900 for 2013/14).

In order to preserve a loss for use against gains in future years, it is necessary to establish that loss. You must return the loss within your Tax Return within four years, or amend an already filed Return to claim the loss. Alternatively, a claim can be made by writing to the tax inspector.

Remember, any size loss if realised in isolation can be used in this way, and could save you 28% tax on the amount of the loss in future years.

Therefore, always claim losses in the year in which they arise and keep a note of the amount of losses you have accumulated.

Registering Your Capital Losses

John sold some shares realising a significant loss of £20,000 in 2009/10, and had no other disposals in the year. He omitted to register the loss at the time.

He is now selling his investment property on which he will realise a significant capital gain. The sale takes place in 2013/14.

In order to utilise the loss, he submits a revised Tax Return for 2009/10 showing the capital loss, which is accepted by HMRC. The loss is carried forward to future years.

He can now use the loss against his capital gain in 2013/14 which saves £5,600 in tax (£20,000 @28%).

59.   Registering Your Rental Losses

If you rent out property then you have an obligation to report the property income and expenses to HMRC (see www.hmrc.gov.uk/report-changes/individual/income.htm#2). You will need to tell HMRC that you are receiving income from property by 5 October after the end of the Tax Year in which the income is received. You may need to complete a tax return, in which case HMRC will notify you of the need to file a Return. However, if you have PAYE earnings, you may be able to have any tax due collected via an adjustment to your PAYE code.

Even if you make a loss it is to your advantage to report this to HMRC. Many people do not realise this and only start reporting the income when they break into profit.

Without reporting the rental losses, you are losing out on being able to set these losses against future income from property, meaning that you will pay more tax than you should.

So if you register these losses now, you will be able to take them forward and offset them in future years.

Registering Your Rental Losses

Harry starts letting out a property in 2006.

For each of the first five years, he calculates a loss of £1,000 per annum and declares this loss on his Tax Return.

Due to changes in mortgage rates and a rise in rental income from the property, he realises a profit of £2,500 in each of the years 2012 and 2013, which he also declares.

Because he has declared the losses in the previous five years, he utilises the losses against the income and saves tax on this income.

Assuming Harry pays tax at 40%, the saving by using the losses is £2,000 (a saving of £1,000 in each year (£2,500 @ 40%)).

Chapter 7.
Capital Allowances

60. Capital Allowances: Annual Investment Allowance

Ensuring that the annual investment allowance (AIA) is claimed on all new items of plant and machinery can save considerable amounts of tax.

The AIA gives a 100% deduction against profits up to the amount of the allowance. The allowance is £250,000 for a temporary period of two years from 1 January 2013, after which it will revert to £25,000 from 1 January 2015.

Where the chargeable accounting period spans 1 January 2013, the allowance is determined pro rata for the period before and after 1 January 2013. The pro rata limits set the maximum AIA expenditure in each period.

Capital Allowances: Annual Investment Allowance

John has a personal company, JKL Ltd, which prepares accounts to 31 March each year. The company incurs capital expenditure of £30,000 in October 2012 and a further £40,000 in February 2013.

In order to determine the maximum AIA that can be claimed, the accounting period must be split into shorter periods – 1 April 2012 to 31 December 2012 (9 months) and 1 January 2013 to 31 March 2013 (3 months).

The pro rata AIA limit for the nine months to 31 December 2012 is £18,750 (9/12 x £25,000).

The pro rata AIA limit for the three months to 31 March 2013 is £62,500 (3/12 x £250,000).

Although the maximum AIA relief available for the year to 31

March 2013 is £81,250, relief for the period 1 April 2012 to 31 December 2012 is capped at £25,000.

For the year to 31 March 2013, he can claim an AIA of £25,000 in respect of the £30,000 of capital expenditure incurred in October 2013 and £40,000 in respect of the expenditure incurred in February 2013 (a total of £65,000).

Although his total AIA limit for the period is £81,250, which exceeds his £70,000 capital expenditure in the period, he cannot claim more than £25,000 for the period from 1 April 2012 to 31 December 2012. His actual expenditure in that period was £30,000 and consequently relief is restricted.

He can therefore claim AIA of £65,000 (£25,000 for the October 2012 expenditure and the full £40,000 of the February 2013 expenditure). He can also claim a writing down allowance for the remainder of the October 2012 expenditure of £5,000.

In certain circumstances it can be more beneficial to claim the writing down allowance rather than the annual investment allowance.

This may be the case, for example, in an unincorporated business where the capital allowance is increasing a loss that is eating into a personal allowance rather than generating a tax rebate.

Claiming the writing down allowance may also be preferable if the intention is to dispose of the asset after a short period of time so as to minimise balancing charges on the disposal.

61. Short Life Assets

Capital items that you expect to keep for no more than eight years from the end of the accounting period in which you acquired them can be treated as short life assets by making a relevant election.

This means the asset is not added to the general capital allowances pool and if disposed of within this period then the loss on scrapping or sale will be realised straight away rather than affecting the general pool.

If the asset is still held after the end of this period then it is automatically added back into the general pool.

Short Life Assets

Graham buys £10,000 worth of new equipment which he thinks will last less than eight years, and hence elects to treat it as a short life asset.

After three years he is proved right when the equipment has passed its useful life and is scrapped, at which point he can claim a balancing allowance for the remainder of his original cost against his profits.

---

62. Write Off Small Pools

The small pools allowance allows you to write off the main or special rate pool or both if the balance on the pool in question is £1,000 or less. This clears the pool in one hit and prevents the need to make minimal capital allowance claims over a number of years.

The small pools allowance can be claimed in respect of new expenditure (usually that remaining after other allowances have been claimed), any brought forward residual balance, less any disposal proceeds of assets which have been sold or otherwise disposed of.

The £1,000 small pools allowance is proportionately reduced for periods of less than 12 months.

Claim Fixed Rate Deductions

Helen incurs expenditure in excess of her AIA limit. The unrelieved balance of £800 is added to her main pool. There is no residual balance bought forward.

As the balance on the pool is less than £1,000, Helen claims the small pools allowance, claiming a writing down allowance for the full £800.

The balance on the main pool is reduced to nil.

63. Choose A Low Emission Car And Claim 100% Allowance

The annual investment allowance is not available in respect of cars. However, it is still possible to obtain a 100% deduction against profits for a car purchased for your business by choosing a car with very low CO_2 emissions. Cars purchased on or after 1 April 2013 and on or before 31 March 2015, qualify for the first-year allowance (FYA) if the emissions are 95g/km or less. Cars purchased before 1 April 2013 qualified for the FYA if the CO_2 emissions were 110g/km or less.

> **Choose A Low Emission Car And Claim 100% First-Year Capital Allowances**
>
> John has a small family business and is looking to buy a company car.
>
> He chooses a car that has CO_2 emissions of 90 g/km and which costs £15,000.
>
> As the car's CO_2 emissions are less than 95 g/km he can claim a 100% FYA thereby obtaining an immediate write-off against profits of £15,000.
>
> If he pays tax at the small profits rate of 20% (financial year 2013) claiming the 100% FYA rather than an 18% WDA will save tax of £2,460 in that year. Choosing a low emission car also minimises the benefit-in-kind tax that John will pay on the company car.

64. Time Your Capital Expenditure

If your cash flow allows it, consider carefully the date on which you invest in new items of plant and machinery or other items qualifying for capital allowances.

A purchase date of a few days either side of your accounting year end date can make all the difference in getting the first capital allowance in this accounting period or having to wait 12 months to get any relief for the expenditure.

> **Time Your Capital Expenditure**
>
> Gordon is considering buying £10,000 worth of equipment for his business.
>
> His year end is 31 March.
>
> By making the purchase prior to the accounting year end date he will be able to claim allowances (either the annual investment allowance or the writing down allowance) a year earlier than if he delayed the purchase until a few days after the year end.
>
> He will receive the tax relief a year earlier.

Chapter 8.
VAT

65.   Should I Register For VAT?

If your taxable turnover is below the VAT threshold then you may not have considered whether registering for VAT could be advantageous for you. The VAT registration threshold is £79,000 from 1 April 2013.

If you incur VAT on supplies and the majority of your customers are registered for VAT, then it may be beneficial to register for VAT on a voluntary basis.

This will allow you to recover the input tax paid on the supplies and also allow you to charge VAT on your invoices.

It will also be beneficial if many of your supplies are zero rated, such as food, as you will be able to reclaim VAT suffered and may receive a VAT repayment each quarter, which is beneficial from a cash-flow perspective.

If you decide to register for VAT then your VAT registered customers will be able to recover the VAT charged on your invoices when they next submit their VAT return.

Registering For VAT

Mark supplies parts to various garages, all of which are registered for VAT.

He pays input tax on all his supplies, and hence would be considerably better off by voluntarily registering for VAT and recovering this input tax.

By registering for VAT, he will also need to charge output tax on his sales.

66. The VAT Cash Accounting Scheme

If your VAT-exclusive turnover is £1.35m or less, then you may account for and pay VAT on the basis of cash paid and received.

You can join this scheme at any time.

Once you are in the scheme you can continue to use it until your taxable turnover exceeds £1.6m per annum.

What this means is that you don't have to pay VAT to HMRC on invoices that have not been paid yet and conversely are not allowed to claim VAT back on expenses you have incurred but not yet paid.

VAT Cash Accounting Scheme

Paul uses the cash accounting scheme as his turnover is below £1.35m per annum.

His major customer is having cash-flow difficulties and, as a result, he is not paid for his invoices totalling £100,000 (net) until nine months after the invoice date, at which time he accounts to HMRC for the VAT due on these.

If he was not using the cash accounting scheme he would have had to account for VAT on an invoice basis and would therefore have been out of pocket to the tune of £20,000 for a period of up to nine months.

This can be enough to bring some businesses down if they do not have sufficient cash to pay this or bank facilities to fund this.

67.   Join The VAT Flat Rate Scheme For Small Businesses

If you are a small business it can be advantageous to join the VAT flat rate scheme for small businesses.

Under the scheme you use a flat rate percentage to work out the amount of VAT you need to pay over to HMRC. You do not need to record VAT on sales and purchases separately and claim the difference. This can save a lot of work.

The flat rate percentage depends on your business sector. The percentages are listed in the HMRC website (see www.hmrc.gov.uk/vat/start/schemes/flat-rate.htm#4). The input tax payable to HMRC is worked out by multiplying the flat rate percentage for the relevant business sector by turnover for the quarter inclusive of VAT.

You can join the scheme as long as your turnover excluding VAT is not more than £150,000 a year. You can stay in the scheme until your turnover reaches £230,000 a year.

More details on the scheme can be found in HMRC Notice 733.

Join The VAT Flat Rate Scheme For Small Businesses

Gill runs a computer repair business. Her annual turnover excluding VAT is £100,000. She registers for the VAT flat rate scheme.

In a particular VAT quarter, her turnover, including VAT, is £31,200. The flat rate percentage for her sector is 10.5%.

She must pay VAT of £3,276 (10.5% x £31,200) over to HMRC.

Chapter 9.
Capital Gains Tax

68. Timing Your Disposals For CGT

A timing advantage of one year on the payment of tax can be achieved simply by delaying sales beyond 5 April in the tax year, so that you have use of the funds for another year and can earn interest on this money for a year longer before having to pay the tax to HMRC.

However, this needs to be balanced against a possible loss of the annual exemption if it has not been fully utilised for the earlier year.

Timing Your Disposals For CGT

Jack is considering selling his investment property. He has already realised gains in excess of his annual exemption.

By delaying the sale of the property until after 5 April, he will pay tax on the gain a year later and can generate some interest income on the money he has put aside for his tax liability.

He will also have the use of the annual exemption for the later tax year to set against the gain.

69. Roll-Over Relief For Business Assets

It is always worth bearing in mind that when you sell certain types of business asset, it is possible to postpone the gain by reinvesting in a qualifying asset for roll-over relief purposes.

This is quite a restricted relief these days and care should be taken before relying on the availability of the relief.

The best feature about this relief is that you can claim it on more than one new purchase, and can include assets purchased one year before to three years after the date of sale of the original asset.

Roll-Over Relief For Business Assets

John sells a qualifying business asset for £100,000, making a gain of £50,000.

He re-invests the entire proceeds into a new qualifying asset and the gain is entirely rolled over into the new asset.

The base cost of the new asset is reduced and capital gains tax payable on the sale of the old asset is postponed.

---

70. Gilts – Tax-Free Capital Gains

Investments in index-linked Government Stocks, British Government Stocks or gild-edged securities (gilts) are exempt from capital gains tax. Index-linked gilts can therefore be attractive, particularly to those paying capital gains at the higher rate of 28%.

Gilts – Tax-Free Capital Gains

Richard buys £50,000 nominal value of 3.5% Stock redeemable in 2013 at a price of £90 per £100 of nominal value.

When the Stock is repaid by the Government, he will make a profit of £5,000, which is completely tax-free.

71. Make A Negligible Value Claim For Worthless Assets

If you own an asset that has become worthless you can make a claim to treat the asset as if you had sold the asset and immediately reacquired it at the time of the claim for its value at that time.

The claim, known as a negligible value claim, enables relief to be given for the loss in value of the asset.

The loss is treated as arising in the year in which the claim is made, or at a time specified in the claim in the two preceding tax years during which time the conditions for the claim were met.

Make A Negligible Value Claim For Worthless Assets

John subscribed for shares in a company. The shares cost £10,000 in 2005. The company failed in October 2013 and the shares became worthless.

John makes a negligible value claim for 2013/14 for the loss on the shares of £10,000. The loss can be set against capital gains. Alternatively, it can be set against his income of 2013/14 or 2012/13 if he has no gains for 2013/14 and does not want to carry the loss forward to set against future capital gains (see Tip 55).

Assuming John is a higher rate taxpayer, the claim will save tax of £2,800 if the loss is offset against capital gains and tax of £4,000 if set against income.

Chapter 10.
Property

72. Utilise Rent-A-Room Relief

If you rent out a room within your own property then you can claim the rent-a-room relief of £4,250.

This can be claimed against the rental income as an alternative to claiming the expenses incurred in letting the room out.

In many cases this eliminates the tax charge entirely, just for ticking a box on the Tax Return form.

It is worth comparing actual costs against this relief to determine whether or not it is more worthwhile to claim the relief rather than the expenses – this will be dependent on the level of expenses compared to the relief, even where the total rental income exceeds the £4,250 threshold.

Where there are two or more sharers renting out rooms, each can claim relief of £2,125. This means that it is possible to earn tax-free rental income under the rent-a-room scheme of more than £4,250 in respect of one property.

Rent-A-Room Relief

<u>Scenario 1 – When it is beneficial to use the relief</u>

Matthew rents out a room in his house for £4,250 per annum, incurring £1,250 in the way of costs, and pays tax on the profit £3,000 of this income at 40%.

He is unaware of rent-a-room relief until he appoints a tax consultant to deal with his tax affairs, and claims it for 2012/13. By making the claim, he saves paying the tax on the £3,000 which is £1,200.

<u>Scenario 2 – When it is not beneficial to use the relief</u>

Luke rents out a room and, after expenses, makes a loss of £1,000 as the rental income is £6,000 and his expenses £7,000.

Clearly here he is better off not making the election, as to do so would turn his £1,000 loss into a profit of £1,750 on which he would incur tax, as under the rent-a-room scheme where income exceeds the £4,250 limit the excess over the limit is taxed (without regard to the expenses).

73.   Furnished Holiday Lettings

Although the tax advantages for furnished holiday lettings have been reduced, they still offer advantages over other types of lettings.

Losses arising from a furnished holiday lettings business can now only be set off against profits from the same furnished holiday lettings business. It is no longer possible to set losses against general income as was the case before 6 April 2011.

As all UK furnished holiday lets by the same person are treated as part of the same FHL business, losses on one property are effectively offset against profits from other properties in the same year. Losses are not restricted to set off against the same property, just the same FHL business.

However, furnished holiday lettings are still treated as a trade and retain some of the advantages.

Capital allowances may be claimed in respect of plant and machinery. Capital gains tax reliefs, such as entrepreneurs' relief and roll-over relief may also be available.

However, to qualify as a furnished holiday letting and to benefit from associated advantages, since 6 April 2012 the minimum period for which the property must be let in a year is 105 days and the period for which it must be available for letting 210 days. Steps must be taken to ensure that these conditions are met.

However, a period of grace election can be made if a property fails to meet the FHL occupancy condition for a year despite a genuine intention to let, providing that the occupancy condition was met in the previous year (either on its own or as the result of an averaging). Making an election allows the property to remain within the regime for one or two years on making a claim. This is worthwhile as it allows time to increase the letting without having to deal with the consequences of becoming a non-holiday let (such as possible balancing charges).

Where a property is let on short term lets, the FHL rules offer advantages over other lets and it is still worthwhile to fall within the FHL regime, despite the restriction on loss relief.

Furnished Holiday Lettings

John buys a house in Brighton, which qualifies as a furnished holiday letting.

He makes a loss in the 2013/14 tax year of £5,000, which he can set against future income from his FHL business.

After three years, he sells the property.

He is able to benefit from the capital gains tax reliefs available for traders, such as roll-over relief and entrepreneur's relief.

74. Claim Your 10% Wear And Tear Allowance

If you let a property furnished, not only does the property normally generate more income, but you can also claim the 10% wear and tear deduction from the gross rentals received.

Many non-represented taxpayers regularly miss out on this very easy relief.

Claim Your 10% Wear And Tear Allowance
Alan buys an investment property and discusses the merits and downsides of letting the property furnished or unfurnished with his tax adviser.
By letting it furnished he obtains a deduction from his gross rents in respect of the wear and tear allowance of £2,000 per annum.
If he pays tax at 40%, this saves £800 in tax annually.

75.   Principal Private Residence Relief (PPR)

Most people are aware of the this relief, which allows you to sell your home without having to pay capital gains tax on any profit that you make.

There are many rules associated with this relief, but it is a very valuable exemption as, for the majority of people, the purchase of their home is the biggest investment they ever make.

Where you own more than one home you can choose which one is your main residence, as long as you are living in the property selected as a home. By making the appropriate election (often known as flipping) it is possible to maximise the benefit of the relief (see Tip 76). Professional advice should be sought prior to making an election.

Principal Private Residence (PPR)

John sells his house in 2013 for £450,000, having purchased the property in 2004 for £375,000. As it is his PPR, no tax is payable on the gain he has made on this property.

76. Choosing Your PPR

Where you have more than one property it is possible to choose which one is your PPR at any given time, provided the property is or has been used as a home. This option is available to everyone – not just MPs. However, a person can only have one PPR at any one time.

By 'flipping' the properties, it is possible to maximise relief and ensure that the last 36 months for each PPR qualify for relief (see Tip 77).

Choosing Your PPR

John has a flat in the city that he bought for £100,000 in April 2000. In April 2003 he buys a family home in the country for £400,000. He lives in the flat in the week and the country home at weekends and during holidays.

He elects for the country home to be his PPR.

He sells the country home in July 2013 for £700,000, buying a larger property nearby. As the property has been his PPR throughout the gain is tax-free.

He also sells the flat in July 2013 to fund the larger property, making a gain of £150,000. He is able to claim PPR in respect of the periods from April 2000 to April 2003 and also for the last 36 months.

Had John not flipped his properties so that his country home was his PPR, he would not have been entitled to PPR on the sale and the gain of £300,000 would have attracted capital gains tax.

Although some of the gain on the flat is taxable, the overall tax bill is much reduced.

---

77.   The Last 36 Months Rule

If a property was at some point your PPR then the last 36 months are exempt from tax.

This means that if you have a second property that you now live in, then you are still entitled to PPR for the last 36 months on the other property.

The Last 36 Months Rule

Tom sells a property he has been renting out for the last eight years. He actually owned it for ten years as he lived in it for the first two years.

When the property is sold he realises a profit of £100,000 before PPR relief.

His actual PPR relief would be 2/10ths of the gain (i.e. the first two years he lived in it), but by using the 36 month rule a further 3/10ths of the gain drops out of charge, leaving him with a gain of £50,000 instead of £80,000.

This provides a tax saving on some £30,000 of gain, or £8,400 in capital gains tax at 28%.

In addition, Tom qualifies for the lettings exemption, further reducing his gain.

78.   Private Lettings Relief

If you rent out a property, which was at one time your PPR, you will qualify for the lettings relief.

This can be worth up to £40,000 against the gain realised on the disposal of a property.

Note that this relief is per person, so if property is held jointly it can attract up to £80,000 relief.

Unrepresented taxpayers frequently miss this relief from their calculation of the chargeable gain on a property where they could have claimed it.

Private Lettings Relief

John and Mary sell their investment property, which has been let out and which at one time used to be their main home.

They qualify for the maximum lettings relief and save paying tax on £80,000 of the gain (£40,000 each). Where capital gains tax is payable at the higher rate of 28%, this results in a tax saving of £22,400.

Chapter 11.
Property

79. IHT And Gifts Out Of Income

There is an exemption for inheritance tax purposes in addition to the £3,000 annual allowance for gifts made out of income on a regular basis.

It is important to establish the regularity of the payments in order to qualify for this relief, so if gifts are made in cash then these should be regular in amount and frequency taking one year with another.

A better way of establishing regular payments may be to take out an investment policy for someone such as your (adult) child with premiums being due on a regular basis.

IHT Gifts Out Of Income

John is 50 and earns £200,000 per year.

He has a son who is 25, who cannot work at present due to ill health.

John, who does not need the majority of his income, wishes to gift his son £50,000 per year, but is worried about the effects this will have on his inheritance tax bill and having to survive seven years for these monies to drop out of his estate.

He establishes a quarterly standing order into his son's account, and writes a letter to his son stating that he intends to gift this amount per annum for as long as he continues to work.

He continues to make the payments until his death in an accident seven years later. As he clearly established the regularity of the payments before his death, the amounts paid to his son are removed from his estate and a substantial tax saving has been achieved.

80. Make A Will

Surprisingly, many people still die intestate (i.e. without a will).

With the ease that wills can now be drafted and the low cost of such services, it makes good sense and can save a lot of needless heartache and stress for those left behind by making a will, not to mention saving a lot of tax.

A simple will gifting all your worldly goods to your spouse or civil partner will avoid IHT on your entire estate, as gifts between spouses/civil partners are exempt from IHT.

Remember, if the nil rate band is not fully used on the first death, the unused percentage is available on the death of the deceased's spouse/civil partner.

Making A Will

Rudolph dies intestate in 2013, leaving an estate valued at £1m. Under the intestacy rules, his wife and their children will each receive a proportion of the estate, resulting in a large IHT bill for the family.

This could easily have been avoided by making a will and leaving all his estate to his spouse or leaving property to his children up to the nil rate band (£325,000) and the remainder to his spouse.

81.   Potentially Exempt Transfers

Inheritance tax is essentially a voluntary tax, in that with proper planning there is no need for your estate to pay any tax on your death.

One of the most useful tools is the potentially exempt transfer, or PET.

Under the PET rules any gift made to an individual is exempt from inheritance tax if you survive seven years from the date of the gift. If you die before seven years have elapsed, the amount charged to tax is calculated on a sliding scale, with a lower amount being taxed the longer you survive after making the gift. It is also possible to protect against the IHT liability in the interim period by taking out decreasing term assurance, which basically covers the reducing IHT liability over the seven years.

Potentially Exempt Transfers (PETs)

Gerald makes PETs to his children, Lucy and Lauren, of £250,000 each in 2007.

Provided he survives until 2014, these gifts will drop out of his estate and he will have saved his estate from paying up to £200,000 on this money.

Chapter 12.
Tax Returns and Administration

82. Submit Your Tax Return Online

By submitting your Tax Return online you have longer to do it.

Returns submitted in paper format must reach HMRC by 31 October after the end of the tax year.

However, if you file your Return online you have until the following 31 January to do it.

A penalty is charged if your Return is submitted late. If you file a paper Return after 31 October the penalty applies. Penalties can easily mount up and the later the Return is filed, the higher the penalty charged.

However, if you miss the paper filing date and file online instead by 31 January you will save yourself a penalty.

Filing online also has the added benefit that your tax is worked out automatically.

To find out more about filing your Tax Return online, visit the HMRC website (www.hmrc.gov.uk/individuals/).

83. File Your Tax Return By 30 December

Although you have until 31 January after the end of the tax year to file your Tax Return, if you file it online by 30 December and the amount of tax that you owe is less than £3,000, you can have the tax you owe collected through your PAYE code, rather than having to pay it in one go by 31 January.

This has considerable cash-flow advantages.

File Your Tax Return By 30 December
Adam files his Tax Return online on 15 December. He pays tax at 40%. He owes tax on income of £1,800 and chooses to have the tax collected through his PAYE code. This delays payment, spreading it throughout the following tax year and saving him from having to make a payment of £720 (£1,800 @ 40%) by 31 January.

84. File Your Tax Return On Time To Avoid Hefty Penalties

Hefty penalties apply to people who fail to file their Tax Return on time and you could pay as much as £1,300 in penalties if you file your Tax Return six months late.

The longer the delay in filing the Return, the higher the penalty that is charged. Paper Returns for 2012/13 must be filed by 31 October 2013 and online Returns must be filed by 31 January 2014.

Where a Return is filed after these dates, a penalty is charged.

The penalty is £100 if the Return is filed one day late, even if you do not owe any tax. If the Return is filed up to three months late, a further penalty of £10 per day is charged to a maximum of £900. If the Return is filed six months late a further penalty of £300 or 5% of the tax due, if higher, is charged.

A further penalty of £300 or 5% of the tax due, if higher, is charged if the Return is still outstanding after 12 months.

File Your Tax Return On Time To Avoid Hefty Penalties

John files his 2011/12 self-assessment Return online in August 2013. The Return was due by 31 January 2013. The tax due was £1,000. The Return was filed more than six months late and John is charged a penalty of £1,300. This could easily have been avoided had John been more organised and filed his Return by the deadline of 31 January 2013.

The penalties apply in addition to interest and surcharges on late-paid tax.

85. Use Rounding In Your Tax Return

If you have income that includes 'pence', round down these figures.

For expenses always round them up.

Multiple figures for one entry cannot be rounded until the final figure is calculated, at which point this figure can be rounded up or down as appropriate.

This may not save you a lot of tax but every little bit helps!

Use Rounding In Your Tax Return
Barry is self-employed and uses 15 boxes in total on his Tax Return.
By rounding, he may save tax on up to £14.85, equating to a saving of £5.94 in tax for a 40% taxpayer. Enough for a drink!

86.   Avoid Unnecessary Interest

By ensuring that you pay any tax on time, you can avoid paying the HMRC non-deductible interest for the late payment of tax.

Avoid Unnecessary Interest

Peter files his Tax Return in March, and discovers that he has a liability of £1,000 for the year, which he paid on 16 March.

Because he paid his tax late, he is liable for:

- interest on the late paid tax,
- a further 5% surcharge because the tax was still unpaid on 28 February.

He could quite easily have avoided the interest charge by paying his tax on time.

87.   Do You Need A Tax Return?

You can save yourself a considerable amount of time, effort and expense if you employ a tax adviser, by finding out whether you still need to complete a Return after changes in your circumstances.

HMRC are keen to reduce their workload in processing self-assessment Returns where they are no longer required and you should review this after any change of circumstances.

Visit the HMRC website at www.hmrc.gov.uk/sa/need-tax-return.htm#1 to see if you need to complete a Tax Return.

Do You Need A Tax Return?

Ryan was self-employed for a few years, but has been an employee on PAYE earning under £30,000 per annum for the past two years.

He has no other sources of income or gains.

As he is sent a Tax Return each year, his accountant duly files this and charges a fee for determining that no tax is due.

By checking with HMRC whether he still needs to file and receiving a response that he is being removed from the obligation to file, he saves himself the time and expense of having to complete the form each year.

88. T/O Below VAT Threshold? Complete These Pages...

If your self-employment turnover is less than the VAT registration threshold (£79,000 for 2013/14) then there is no need to go to the trouble and expense of completing the full Self-Employment Supplementary pages (SA103F) and detailing all your expenses.

Instead you can complete the short Self-Employment Supplementary pages (SA103S; available on the HMRC website at www.hmrc.gov.uk/forms/sa103s.pdf), which is only two pages long and save time by entering total expenses in box 19 rather than providing details of specific expenses.

To make life easier, HMRC have issued briefer easy-to-read notes for the key Tax Return pages for 2012/13 returns, including SA103S.

Turnover Less Than The VAT Threshold? Complete These Pages...

Bill sets up in self-employment and commences to trade on 6 April 2012.

His total turnover is £20,000 to 31 March 2013 and hence he can save time and money by only completing the short self-employment pages (SA103S).

89. Check Your Tax Code

Your tax code determines how much tax is deducted under PAYE. You should always check that your tax code is correct as errors may result in too much or too little tax being deducted. Revised codes are sent out automatically after a Tax Return has been submitted and these essentially assume that taxpayer's circumstances remain the same. This may not be the case. For example if you declare untaxed interest on your Tax Return, the auto coding process will assume that you have this income in the following year and adjust the code accordingly. If this is not the case, you will find that you have more tax deducted under PAYE than you need to.

HMRC may also adjust the code to collect tax on savings income. This may be easier than paying it at the end of the tax year, but is not for everyone. You do not need to have this collected through your code. Instead you can ask HMRC to take the savings adjustment out of your code and pay the tax under the self-assessment system. This will increase your take home pay each month.

Where an individual's income is over £100,000 the personal allowance is reduced by £1 for every £2 of income above £100,000. Where HMRC expect the allowance to be abated on the basis that the previous year's income was in excess of £100,000, they will take away the personal allowance from the tax code. If your income is likely to be less than £100,000 you can ask that they readjust the code, rather than waiting until you do your Tax Return to claim a repayment. This will provide a cash-flow advantage.

If you do not think your code is right or it includes items that you would rather were dealt with via self-assessment, you need to contact HMRC. They should amend the code.

Check Your Tax Code

Darren has a company car.

In April 2013 he changed his car to a more environmentally friendly model.

As replacement cars do not now need to be notified to HMRC on form P46 (Car) (although employers can provide HMRC with this information online if they want to), HMRC may not be aware of the change until his P11D for 2013/14 is submitted in July 2014.

Darren's tax code for 2013/14 is based on his previous car and consequently Darren pays more tax than he needs to each month as a result.

By checking his tax code and telling HMRC about the change, he will have more take-home pay each month.

90. Payments On Account

If your total net tax liability for the year is less than £1,000, or if at least 80% of the total tax due for the year is covered by tax deducted at source, then you do not need to make payments on account for the following tax year.

The second test is sometimes missed by HMRC and people are asked to make payments on account unnecessarily, resulting in a loss of the use of the money unnecessarily early.

Payments On Account

Robert calculates his tax liability at £7,000 for the year 2012/13, of which £1,200 relates to investment income payable under self-assessment. The remainder (£5,800) was deducted under PAYE.

Because his net tax liability is over the £1,000 limit, he assumes he has to make payments on account for the following year and hence enters these figures onto his Tax Return.

However, as over 80% of his total tax liability is deducted at source under PAYE, he meets the second test and does not need to make payments on account. The tax on his investment income is payable in full by 31 January following the end of the tax year. By being aware of this test, he avoids making payments on account and benefits from the associated cash-flow advantage.

91. Watch Out For The Online Tax Calculation...

Where the Tax Return is submitted online, the associated tax calculation shows the tax due for the year, not the balance which needs to be paid.

Where payments on account have been made during the year, these need to be deducted from the liability for the year to show the balance due, if any, for the year of the Return.

It is only this balance, plus the first payment on account for the following year, that needs to be paid by 31 January after the end of the tax year.

Chapter 13.
Some Final Tips

92.   Income From A Family Trust

If you have a family trust with discretionary powers, consider making payments to your children.

Trusts are a complex area and advice should always be sought but it is possible to utilise the children's tax-free personal allowance in this way.

In fact, these payments can be combined with the pension payments in respect of your children (see Tip 17) to make a double saving.

Income From A Family Trust

Andrew's family has a family trust, and it makes payments net of the trust rate of tax (45%) equivalent to the annual personal allowance of £9,440 gross per annum (2013/14 figures).

The tax of £4,248 paid by the trust is recovered by the children, by making a repayment claim. An amount of £2,880 net (£3,600 gross) is paid into a pension scheme on their behalf, resulting in a further tax advantage of £720 per child.

93. Children's Income

Income earned from gifts from parents is exempt if less than £100 per annum. Otherwise the income is taxable as that of the parents.

Consider gifting sufficient capital to generate this amount in income or utilise tax-exempt savings products to build up savings for the children.

This limit can be overcome by putting money into a Junior ISA (see Tip 8) or by investing in Children's Bonds, which generate a tax-free return.

Gifts can be made by grandparents to grandchildren without restriction.

Children's Income

John is a higher rate taxpayer (paying tax at 40%) and gifts each of his children £2,000, which is placed in a children's account for them and earns £80 interest per annum. As this is less than £100 it is not taxed as John's income. John therefore saves £32 per annum in tax which he would have otherwise paid on the interest income had the money been placed in an account in his own name.

94. Children And Gifts Of Capital

Although income from gifts from parents is treated as that of the parents if it exceeds £100 per annum, gifts from other relatives do not suffer this treatment.

Therefore to save some tax and utilise your children's personal allowances, ask your relatives to gift your children money and you can do likewise for their children (although ensure there is not a connection between one gift and another).

Children And Gifts Of Capital

John's mother gifts his children £3,000 per annum to utilise her IHT exemption.

The income generated by this gift is covered by the children's personal allowances, and hence tax is saved as a result.

The children can complete form R85 to receive the interest tax-free.

95. Distributions From Trusts

As trusts suffer from a 45% tax charge on their income (2013/14 rates), it is well worth the trustees considering making income distributions to those on the basic or 40% rates of tax. This action will generate a tax refund in the beneficiaries' hands.

Distribution From Trusts

Jay is a beneficiary of his Grandmother's Trust, and for 2013/14 has other income of £10,000.

The trustees can make a distribution to him of £11,000, which is £20,000 net of 45% trust tax. He can reclaim the difference between the trust rate (45%) and the basic rate (20%), i.e. 25%, equivalent to a tax refund of £5,000.

96.   Making The Most Of A Low Income Year

You may find yourself within a tax year and know that your income is going to be substantially lower, perhaps as a deliberate move by yourself through your company or as an employee between jobs.

This can present a good opportunity to realise gains or make surrenders on single premium bonds or other investments you have.

> **Making The Most Of A Low Income Year**
>
> Josh is an employee and earns £150,000 per annum.
>
> He is made redundant from his job, and is forced to take 12 months off as part of his redundancy deal. His redundancy pay is taxed in 2012/13 and provides him with sufficient income to live on for 12 months.
>
> He will not have any income in 2013/14.
>
> He can take this opportunity to realise capital gains and to take advantage of the lower 18% rate of capital gains tax.
>
> The first £10,900 of any gains for 2013/14 is covered by his annual exemption for the year. Gains realised in excess of the annual exemption are taxed at 18% to the extent that total income and gains does not exceed £32,010 (2013/14 figures) and at 28% thereafter.

97. Farmers' Averaging

Farmers are permitted by election to average their profits over two tax years on a rolling basis.

This can be especially useful where one year is particularly good followed by a particularly bad one.

Farmers' Averaging

Ian is a farmer. His profit for 2012/13 was £12,000 and his profit for 2013/14 is £50,000.

By making the election, his average profit for each of the two years becomes £31,000.

He therefore avoids the higher rate tax at 40% which would otherwise be payable on his better year.

This means that he has an overall tax saving.

98. Authors, Composers And Other Creative Artists

The same concept as for farmers' averaging also applies for authors, composers and other creative artists to help them improve their tax position.

Authors, Composers And Other Creative Artists

Patrick is an author.

The sales on his last book have slowed down and his income from sales of the book is £10,000 in 2012/13.

He launches his new book in September 2013 to much critical acclaim, and generates a profit of £60,000 in 2013/14.

By utilising averaging, his average profit for each of the two years becomes £35,000 and he avoids the higher rate tax that would otherwise be payable on his good year and saves tax overall.

99. Keeping Your Child Benefit

The High Income Child Benefit Charge applies from 7 January 2013 where either a person in receipt of child benefit or his or her live-in partner (whether or not they are married or in a civil partnership) has income of £50,000 or more.

The charge is set at 1% of the child benefit awarded for each £100 by which income exceeds £50,000. Where income is £60,000 or more, the charge will equal the child benefit paid in the year.

Where the recipient does not live with a partner and has income of £50,000 or more a year, it is the recipient who will pay the charge. However, where a couple live together, if only one person has income in excess of £50,000 that person will pay the charge. Where both parties have income in excess of £50,000 the person with the higher income will pay the charge. This means the person paying the income tax charge will not necessarily be the same person who receives the benefit.

It is possible for a couple each earning £49,999 (a total income of £99,998) to retain full child benefit, whereas a single person or a household with a single earner with an income of £60,000 will have to repay all the child benefit.

Where one partner has income of more than £50,000, redistributing income may enable the couple to retain their child benefit. Similarly, in a single parent household where income exceeds £50,000, reducing income to below £50,000 by, say, delaying payments, entering into a salary sacrifice or contributing to a pension, may allow child benefit to be retained in full. Keeping income below £60,000 if it is not possible to reduce income to below £50,000 will mean at least not all child benefit is clawed back.

Those affected by the child benefit tax can choose not to receive the benefit or can continue to receive it but pay it back in tax.

Keeping Your Child Benefit

Henry and Paula both work in the family business. They have two children and receive child benefit of £1,752 a year (2013/14 rates).

Henry has income of £65,000 and Paula has income of £25,000. The child benefit is paid to Paula. However, as Henry's income is above £60,000, from 7 January 2013 he suffers an income tax charge equal to the full amount of the child benefit paid to Paula.

By reducing Henry's income to £45,000 and increasing Paula's income to £45,000, the high income child benefit charge does not apply and they are able to keep the full amount of their child benefit. At current rates this will make them £1,752 a year better off, despite the fact that their combined income is unchanged. They will also save tax because some income will be taxed at the basic rate rather than at the higher rate (see Tip 6).

100. Paying A Bonus To Increase SMP

Statutory maternity pay (SMP) is paid at a rate of 90% of average weekly earnings for the first six weeks and at the standard rate (£136.78 for 2013/14) for the remainder of the maternity pay period (or at a rate of 90% of average weekly earnings if less).

Paying a bonus in the period over which average weekly earnings are calculated will increase the employee's average weekly earnings and therefore the SMP payable in the first six weeks.

Small employers (total annual NIC bill of £45,000 or less) can recover 103% (2013/14 rate) of any SMP paid, so the additional SMP paid to the employee does not cost the employer extra.

Paying A Bonus To Increase SMP

Sam has his own company and employs his daughter Jayne. She is expecting her first baby. Her average weekly earnings, based on her normal salary, are £500 per week. She is due a bonus of £2,400.

By paying her the bonus during the set period, the bonus is taken into account in calculating her average weekly earnings.

As a result, her average weekly earnings are increased to £800 per week. This increases the SMP payable in the first six weeks of her maternity leave from £450 per week (90% of £500) to £720 per week (90% of £800).

Sam can reclaim the SMP paid.

101. **Take Your Tax-Free Lump Sum**

By taking the lump sum option offered on most personal pension schemes you receive a tax-free lump sum and purchase an annuity with the balance.

Because the annuity is taxable whereas the lump sum is not (as long as it does not exceed 25% of the pension fund), you can be considerably better off from a tax viewpoint by taking the lump sum.

Take Your Tax-Free Lump Sum

Upon retirement Alex is offered the choice of:

- a straightforward annuity for his pension fund of £100,000 of £6,000 per year, or

- a lump sum of £25,000 and an annuity of £5,000 per year.

By taking the latter lump sum option he saves tax yearly on the amount of the annuity forgone.

He also has the opportunity to invest the lump sum to generate additional income (although any income earned may be taxable in its own right depending on the nature of the investment).

---

102. BONUS TIP... Claim Your Pre-Trading Expenditure

Many people are not aware that you can claim expenses incurred in the seven years before commencement of trading against your first year's trading profits.

The expenses are treated as having been incurred on the first day of trading.

The rules for determining whether a pre-trading expense is deductible mirror those for expenses generally. For a pre-trading expense to be allowable it must have been incurred wholly and exclusively for the purposes of the trade.

Make sure you keep all receipts for expenses incurred in this way.

Claim For Pre-Trading Expenditure

Adrian has incurred pre-trading expenses of over £5,000 and has kept all his receipts for these expenses, which are all qualifying expenses.

As a result, his profit in his first year of self-employment is lowered by £5,000. A 45% taxpayer would save £2,250 in tax, a 40% taxpayer, £2,000 in tax and a basic rate taxpayer £1,000 in tax.

So once again, make sure you keep all those receipts as you could make a very significant tax saving.

A Final Word.....

CONGRATULATIONS.....you have managed to read through all the tips.

Hopefully by reading through these practical tips you will have come across at least a few that will apply to your circumstances and save you some tax.

Or at the very least they have given you food for thought and you will take some professional advice before taking any action or refraining from any action as a result of reading these tips.

The tips are for guidance only and professional advice should always be sought before undertaking tax planning of any sort as individual circumstances vary and other considerations may have to be taken into account before acting on these tips.

There are always more tips as tax is a very complex subject.

However I have tried to cover the more practical ideas within this book in the hope that each and every one of you acquiring this guide can take something from it.

Happy Tax Savings!

Lightning Source UK Ltd.
Milton Keynes UK
UKOW05f1921260114

225278UK00001B/15/P

9 780957 613904